DIY FOR BOYS

THE HALLOWEEN GROSS-OUT GUIDE

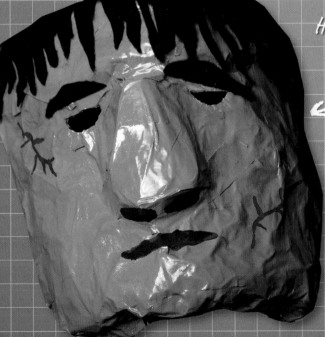

Halloween mask

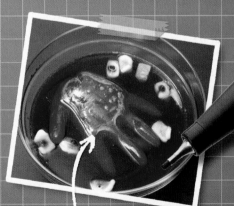

Icy body-parts punch

by Ruth Owen

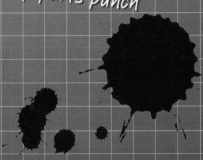

PowerKiDS press

New York

Published in 2014 by The Rosen Publishing Group, Inc.
29 East 21st Street, New York, NY 10010

Produced for Rosen by Ruby Tuesday Books Ltd
Editor for Ruby Tuesday Books Ltd: Mark J. Sachner
US Editor: Joshua Shadowens
Designer: Emma Randall

With special thanks to Steve Owen for his help in developing and making
the projects in this book.

Photo Credits:
Cover, 1, 5, 7, 8, 10—11, 12—13, 14—15, 16—17, 18—19, 20—21, 22—23, 24—25,
26—27, 28—29 © Ruby Tuesday Books and John Such; cover, 1, 3, 4—5, 6, 9,
10—11, 12—13, 18—19, 22, 25, 26 © Shutterstock.

Library of Congress Cataloging-in-Publication Data

Owen, Ruth, 1967—
 The Halloween gross-out guide / Ruth Owen.
   pages cm — (DIY for boys)
 Includes index.
 ISBN 978-1-4777-6290-5 (library binding) — ISBN 978-1-4777-6291-2 (pbk.) —
 ISBN 978-1-4777-6292-9 (6-pack)
 1. Handicraft—Juvenile literature. 2. Halloween decorations—Juvenile
literature. I. Title.
 TT900.H32O94 2014
 745.594'1646—dc23
                              2013035045

Manufactured in the United States of America

CPSIA Compliance Information: Batch #W14PK8 For Further Information contact: Rosen Publishing, New York, New York at 1-800-237-9932

CONTENTS

WARNING!

Neither the author nor the publisher shall be liable for any bodily harm or damage to property that may happen as a result of carrying out the projects in this book.

A DIY HALLOWEEN

For about 2,000 years, people have been celebrating Halloween on October 31. For the **Celtic** people of Ireland, Britain, and France, this date was their New Year's Eve.

As summer ended, and the winter season of darkness began, the Celts believed that on October 31, the barriers between the human world and the **spirit** world were at their weakest. On this night, the ghosts of the dead would return to Earth and roam among humans. Today, we still celebrate all things ghostly on this date by dressing up and having parties.

This year, as always, stores everywhere will be filled with Halloween goods. Why not "do it yourself," though, and make all the things you need from fake blood to Halloween masks, gruesome green slime to frozen body parts!

STICKY FAKE BLOOD

If you are planning to spend this Halloween dressed as a blood-sucking **vampire** or flesh-eating **zombie**, you will need to get your hands on lots of blood. Fake blood that is!

You can buy fake blood from costume stores, but it's much more fun to create your own. The ingredients used in this fake blood recipe are probably already in your kitchen, and when combined, they produce a blood mixture that looks just like the real thing.

So this year, get mixing and make your own sticky, drippy blood to complete your gruesome Halloween costume.

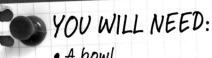

YOU WILL NEED:

- A bowl
- Measuring spoons
- A spoon for mixing
- Corn syrup
- Flour
- Red and blue food coloring
- An eye dropper
- Water (if required)
- A small jar or container for storing your blood

STEP 1:

Using the measuring spoons, place 1 teaspoon of flour, 4 teaspoons of corn syrup, and half a teaspoon of red food coloring in a bowl.

STEP 2:

Thoroughly mix the three ingredients until they are blended and smooth.

At this point, the fake blood mix will look bright red and not very realistic.

STEP 3:
To create a true, dark, blood-red color, you need to add the tiniest amount of blue food coloring. Start by adding just two or three tiny drops of blue using the eye dropper. Mix thoroughly.

Blue food coloring

STEP 4:
Keep adding small drops of blue until the color of the blood mix looks realistic.

Remember: You can add more blue, but you can't take it back out if you put in too much at the start.

STEP 5:
You can store your fake blood in an airtight jar in the refrigerator until you need to use it. If you want your blood to be stickier and thicker, add more flour. To make your blood more drippy, mix in a little water.

WARNING:
Some food colorings stain clothes and surfaces. So wear old clothes with your fake blood, or test the fake blood for staining before adding it to your costume or dripping it onto carpet!

Using flour, water, some make-up, and fake blood, you can create a **gory** wound to top off your horrifying Halloween look.

Movie make-up artists train and practice for years to gain the skills to create realistic-looking wounds and other injuries. So it's worth practicing your horror movie make-up skills ahead of the big day. Then you'll be ready to gross-out your friends by showing up to the festivities with a stomach-churning, bloody cut on your face, arm, or hand!

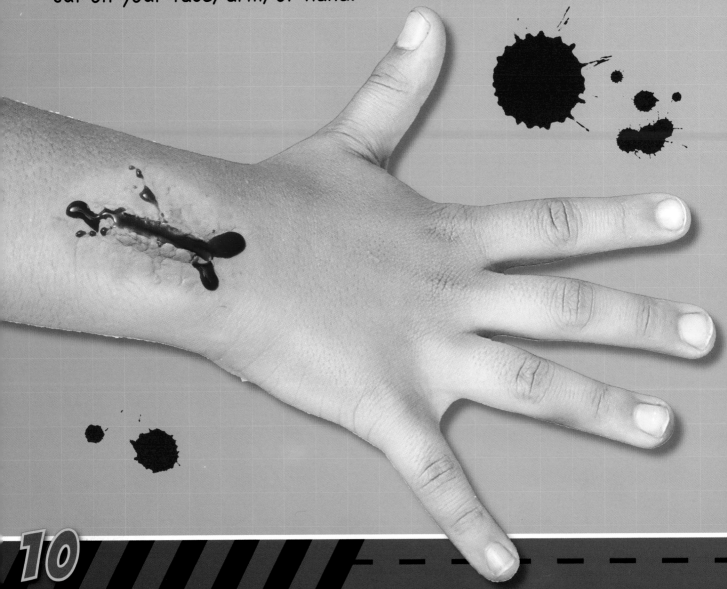

YOU WILL NEED:

- A bowl
- A spoon for mixing
- Flour
- Water
- Measuring spoons
- A sheet of paper
- White glue
- A paintbrush
- A butter knife
- Liquid foundation make-up (in a color that matches your skin)
- Face powder (in a color that matches your skin)
- A make-up sponge and brush
- Fake blood (see pages 6–9)
- A triangular piece of clear plastic from a food carton

STEP 1:

Mix 2 tablespoons of flour with a teaspoon of water. You need to create some dough that is soft enough to mold with your fingers, but is not sticky. Add more flour or water as needed.

Thicker, raised dough in center

Flat edges

STEP 2:

When the dough is ready, roll it into a short sausage shape using your hands. Then, start to flatten the sausage onto a sheet of paper. Smooth out the edges of the dough, but leave a raised area in the center.

STEP 3:

Allow the dough skin to dry a little and firm up for about an hour.

STEP 4:

Mix a teaspoon of white glue with a teaspoon of water. Paint some glue mixture onto your arm. Peel the dough skin off the paper and lay it over the glue on your arm. Allow the glue to dry before continuing with the next stages.

Make a cut

STEP 5:

Using the blunt edge of a butter knife, make a long cut in the raised part of the dough skin. You can peel back and mold the edges of the cut to make it look more realistic.

STEP 6:

Using a make-up sponge, cover the wound with liquid foundation make-up. Smooth the make-up onto the skin on your arm to help blend the dough skin with your real skin.

Wound dusted with face powder

Fake blood

STEP 7:

Using a make-up brush or sponge, dust the wound and surrounding skin with face powder.

STEP 8:

Trickle fake blood into the wound.

STEP 9:

Finally, if you wish, press a "jagged" piece of see-through plastic into the wound to look like a shard of glass.

MAKE A MASK

Hundreds of years ago, people believed that on the night of October 31, the spirits of the dead roamed the Earth.

On that spookiest of nights, if people left their homes, they dressed up so the wandering spirits would think they were fellow ghosts and not know they were human. To make themselves look like spirits, people put ash on their faces or wore masks.

Today, we still like to wear costumes and masks at Halloween. At this time of year, stores are filled with cool costumes to buy, but this year, why not try making and decorating your own Halloween mask made from **papier-mâché**.

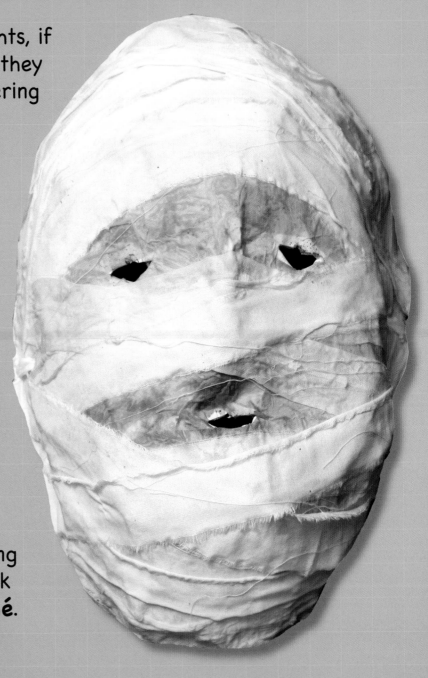

YOU WILL NEED:

- Thick aluminum foil
- A balloon
- Tape
- A bowl
- A newspaper
- White glue (mixed three parts glue to one part water)
- A paintbrush
- Cardboard
- A craft knife
- Paints, fabric scraps, and your choice of materials for decorating the mask

STEP 1:
You may need a helper to assist you with Step 1. Take a large piece of foil and place it over your face. Gently press the foil around your head and into your face's features to create a mold of your face.

STEP 2:
Roughly trim off any excess foil to create a mask shape, and then tape your foil face to an inflated balloon to make it more sturdy to work with.

STEP 3:
Tear the newspaper into strips about 1 inch (2.5 cm) wide.

Foil mold of face

Balloon

Stand the balloon in a bowl to keep the mold as upright as you can.

STEP 4:

Using the paintbrush, gently brush some glue onto the foil mask. Lay a strip of newspaper onto the glue, and then brush more glue over the top. Repeat this with more strips, slightly overlapping each strip, until the mask is covered. Allow the papier-mâché to dry for 24 hours.

STEP 5:

If you wish to add a specially-shaped nose to your mask, make the shape from cardboard and tape it to the mask when the papier-mâché is dry.

STEP 6:

Repeat Step 4. If you have added a cardboard nose, cover this with papier-mâché, too. Allow the second layer of papier-mâché to dry for 24 hours. Then your mask is ready to decorate!

Cut out the eye holes using a craft knife.

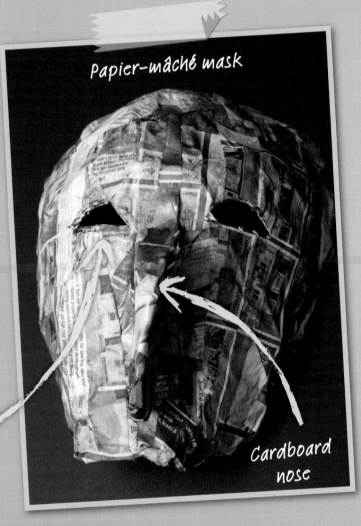

Papier-mâché mask

Cardboard nose

STEP 7:

To make a mummy mask, soak paper towels in cold coffee and allow them to drip dry. Tear the towels into strips and glue to the mask to look like ancient skin. Tear thin, white fabric into strips and glue on for bandages.

MUMMY MASK

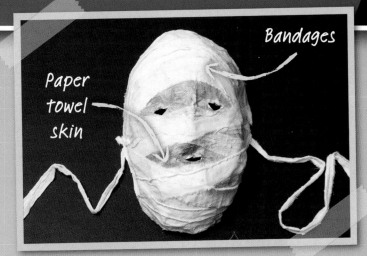

Bandages

Paper towel skin

Old scraps of white fabric

STEP 8:
To secure the mask to your head, cut a small hole in each side of the mask and thread through elastic, string, or fabric strips.

Paper towels soaked in cold coffee

FRANKENSTEIN'S MONSTER MASK

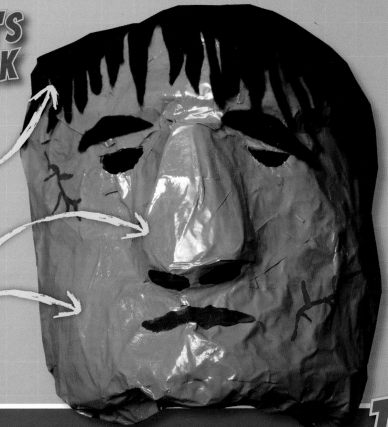

Black felt glued on for hair

Large cardboard nose

Green paint

17

ALIEN NIGHT LIGHTS

This Halloween, raise the fear factor at your party by not only having jack-o'-lanterns to light the darkness, but also some creepy alien night lights.

Many people say they have seen these gray-skinned visitors from outer space. They describe the terrifying **extraterrestrials** as having huge heads and large **menacing** eyes.

With just some balloons, old newspapers, and green cellophane, you can create your own papier-mâché alien visitors with spooky, shining eyes. Place your aliens in dark corners of the house or yard, and truly freak out your friends!

YOU WILL NEED:

- Newspapers
- A balloon
- A bowl
- Cooking oil
- White glue (mixed three parts glue to one part water)
- A paintbrush
- A craft knife
- Gray and white spray paint
- A black marker
- Scissors
- Green cellophane
- Tape
- An LED tealight or small flashlight for each alien head

STEP 1:

Tear the newspaper into strips about 1 inch (2.5 cm) wide.

STEP 2:

Blow up a balloon. If you wish, you can stand the balloon in a bowl to keep it upright as you work. Smear the balloon with cooking oil to stop the papier-mâché from sticking to it.

STEP 3:

Using the paintbrush, gently brush some glue onto the balloon. Lay a strip of newspaper onto the glue, and then brush more glue over the top. Repeat this with more strips, slightly overlapping each strip, until the balloon is covered. Allow the papier-mâché to dry for 24 hours.

Papier-mâché

Balloon

STEP 4:
Repeat Step 3, then allow the second layer of papier-mâché to dry for 24 hours.

STEP 5:
Using a craft knife, trim the bottom, or neck area, of the papier-mâché head so that it has a smooth straight edge that allows the head to stand up. As you cut the papier-mâché, the balloon inside will pop, and can be removed. Make sure the neck hole is large enough to get your hand inside it.

STEP 6:
Draw the outlines of the alien's eyes onto the papier-mâché head, and cut them out.

Cut out the eyes.

Trim a straight edge here.

STEP 7:
Spray paint the outside of the head gray. Carefully spray paint the inside of the head with white paint to cover the newspaper. Allow the paint to dry.

STEP 8:
Using a marker, draw on the alien's nose and mouth.

STEP 9:
Cut two pieces of green cellophane that are slightly larger than the eye holes.

STEP 10:
Using glue or tape, stick a piece of cellophane behind each eye inside the head.

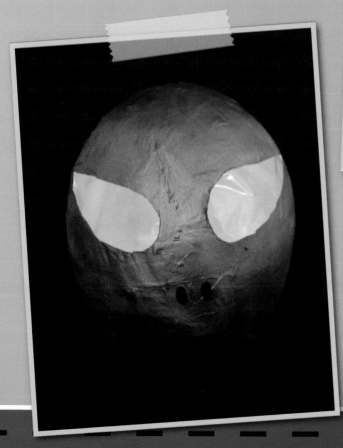

LED tealight

STEP 11:
Stand the alien head over an LED tealight or small flashlight, and your creepy alien night light is complete!

AWESOME SLIME

Halloween just wouldn't be complete without some gooey, slurpy, rubbery slime!

This cool slime recipe is easy to make. You can even try experimenting with the quantities of the different ingredients to create runnier slime or firmer slime.

Use food colorings to make batches of slime in different colors. Of course, it goes without saying, that green slime is by far the best!

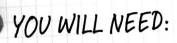

YOU WILL NEED:

- 2 bowls
- 2 spoons for mixing
- Measuring cups
- Measuring spoons
- Water
- Borax powder (from the laundry aisle in a supermarket)
- White glue
- Food coloring

STEP 1:

In one bowl, mix 1 teaspoon of borax powder with 1 cup of water. Stir until the borax completely dissolves.

STEP 2:

In the second bowl, mix half a cup of white glue, half a cup of water, and some food coloring.

Glue, water, and green food coloring

Blended glue, water, and green food coloring

STEP 3:

Mix the glue, water, and food coloring until it is smooth and completely blended.

STEP 4:

Add more food coloring at this stage, if you wish, to create a stronger color.

STEP 5:

Now pour the borax and water mixture from the first bowl into the second bowl, stirring all the time.

STEP 6:

The mixture will immediately start to stiffen and turn from liquid to a rubbery consistency.

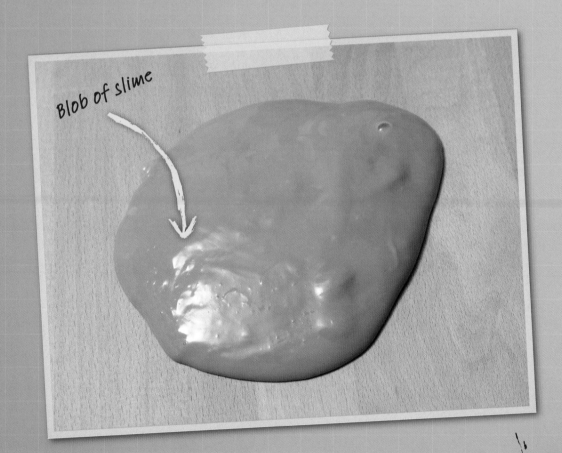

Blob of slime

STEP 7:

As the slime mixture becomes rubbery, dive in with your hands and squeeze and pound the mixture until you have a big blob of slime!

STEP 8:

Now you can play with your slime, have slime fights with your friends, or drape it around the house as a truly disgusting Halloween decoration!

Store your slime in a plastic sandwich baggie to keep it from drying out.

WARNING:

Some types of food coloring can stain clothes and surfaces. Before playing with your slime around the house, check that it doesn't leave yucky, green stains behind.

ICY BODY-PARTS PUNCH

When you offer your party guests something to drink this Halloween, make sure it's a fizzy, fruity **punch** that's swimming with gruesome icy body parts!

You can research recipes for punch online, or try mixing your favorite sodas and fruit juices. You can even just fill the punch bowl with soda. A red or green soda looks particularly gruesome.

Your Halloween guests won't care what they are drinking because they will be blown away by the icy eyeballs and **severed** hand that's floating in their drink!

YOU WILL NEED:

- Water
- Food coloring
- A jug
- Rubber gloves
- String
- Scissors
- Ice cube trays
- Candy and blueberries
- A punch bowl
- Punch

STEP 1:

To make the severed hand, mix food coloring with water in a jug.

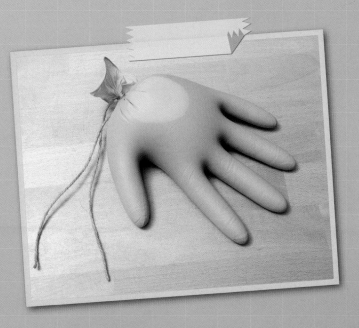

STEP 2:

If the glove is the kind that has talcum powder inside, turn the glove inside it. Then pour the colored water into the glove. Tightly tie a piece of string around the glove to seal it and place the glove in the freezer for 24 hours.

STEP 3:

To make eyeballs, use chewy candy that comes in a doughnut shape or a white blob. Then push a blueberry into the center of the candy to make it look like an eyeball.

You can buy other candy body parts, such as brains and teeth, to float in your punch, too.

Eyeballs

STEP 4:

Place the candy eyeballs into ice cube trays and cover with water. Put the eyeballs into the freezer for 24 hours.

STEP 5:

When you are ready to serve your guests a drink, pour the punch into a punch bowl.

STEP 6:

To remove the icy severed hand from the glove, make a small cut in the glove and then carefully peel the glove from the hand. Place the hand in the punch.

STEP 7:

Gently tap the icy eyeballs from the ice cube tray and float them in the punch.

ENJOY!

GLOSSARY

Celtic (KEL-tik)
Related to or having to do with the religions, languages, and cultures of people and tribes who lived in parts of modern-day Europe.

extraterrestrials (ek-struh-tuh-RES-tree-ulz)
Creatures from outer space.

gory (GOR-ee)
Covered in blood and horrible to look at.

menacing (MEH-nuh-sing)
Threatening or frightening.

papier-mâché (pay-per-mah-SHAY)
A material made from newspapers and glue that can be molded when it is wet. It hardens as it dries, so it can be used for making models and sculptures.

punch (PUNCH)
A drink made from a mixture of different ingredients, such as fruit juice and soda. Punch is usually served in small cups from a large bowl.

severed (SEH-vurd)
Sliced or cut through.

spirit (SPIR-ut)
Having to do with a world or realm that is not physical and may be represented by ghosts and other supernatural forms.

vampire (VAM-pyr)
A person who is dead, but is able to rise from his or her grave to suck the blood of living people.

zombie (ZOM-bee)
A dead body that is able to climb from its grave and move around. Zombies appear to be in a trance. Sometimes, zombies are said to eat the flesh of humans!

WEBSITES
Due to the changing nature of Internet links, Powerkids Press has developed an online list of websites related to the subject of this book. This site is updated regularly. Please use this link to access the list:
www.powerkidslinks.com/dfb/hallow/

READ MORE

Ipcizade, Catherine. *How to Make Frightening Halloween Decorations*. Halloween Extreme. Mankato, MN: Capstone Press, 2011.

Lynette, Rachel. *Let's Throw a Halloween Party!* Holiday Parties. New York. PowerKids Press, 2011.

Skillicorn, Helen. *Spooky Crafts*. Creative Crafts for Kids. New York: Gareth Stevens, 2010.

INDEX